Monetary

vs.

Fiscal Policy

The Seventh Annual Arthur K. Salomon Lecture
THE GRADUATE SCHOOL OF BUSINESS ADMINISTRATION
NEW YORK UNIVERSITY

Monetary

vs.

Fiscal Policy

Milton Friedman

&

Walter W. Heller

W · W · Norton & Company · Inc ·

NEW YORK

Contents

Foreword

The Graduate School of Business Administration of New York University considers that one of its important missions is to provide a forum for the exchange of new ideas and knowledge which may affect the community and the country.

As we prepared for the Seventh Annual Arthur K. Salomon Lecture on November 14, 1968, we decided to vary our format in an election year by having two speakers on the program instead of one as in previous years. In light of the fact that a new administration would be chosen eight days before the lecture, it was our purpose to present a meaningful dialogue on a significant economic issue of the future.

Therefore, we invited two well-known apostles of economics with widely divergent viewpoints to present their opinions on what each considered the most appropriate means to stabilize the economy.

Professor Milton Friedman, the leading spokesman for the monetarist school of thought, was asked to comment on the monetary policy which he considers necessary to accomplish economic stabilization, and Professor Walter W. Heller, the nation's foremost advocate of the neo-Keynesian economics, was called upon to discuss the importance of fiscal policy as an approach to this problem.

Since each man could easily be identified with one or the other of the presidential candidates, we hoped that their confrontation would give some indication of the economic philosophy likely to affect, at least to some degree, the monetary and fiscal policies. In addition, the choice of these two outstanding economists to appear for the first time anywhere in a public debate would—we were confident—attract nationwide attention in the world of business and finance.

The response exceeded our expectations. Not only was the lecture hall filled to capacity, but an overflow audience had to be served by closed-circuit television installed in several classrooms. Virtually all media gave the lecture extensive coverage and the response by the press, TV, and radio surpassed any that we had received at previous lectures in the series.

Space does not permit us to enumerate at length the activities, honors, and accomplishments of the two men who shared our platform. Each is an authority on economics and related disciplines. Each is active in research agencies and in learned societies. Dr. Milton Friedman is the Paul Snowden Russell Distinguished Service Professor of Economics at the University of Chicago. Dr. Walter W. Heller is Regents' Professor of Economics at the University of Minnesota.

In 1967, Dr. Friedman was elected president of the American Economics Association, which previously had given him the John Bates Clark Medal. He has been an economic adviser to presidential nominee Barry Goldwater and to President Richard M. Nixon. Author of many books and articles on economics, he writes a column for *Newsweek* magazine.

Dr. Heller was appointed chairman of the President's Council of Economic Advisers by President John F. Kennedy and remained in that capacity until late in 1964. Later, he served as consultant to the Executive Office of the President during Lyndon B. Johnson's Administration. A widely published author, Dr. Heller is considered the principal economic spokesman for Keynesian economic policies. Dr. Friedman, on the other hand, is considered one of the principal critics of such economic policies.

The Friedman-Heller lecture, as presented in these pages, includes some revisions of the verbal exchange. Notes and a glossary of terms and references have been added for the convenience of the reader.

JOSEPH H. TAGGART
DEAN OF THE GRADUATE SCHOOL
OF BUSINESS ADMINISTRATION,
EXECUTIVE DEAN OF THE SCHOOLS
OF BUSINESS, NEW YORK UNIVERSITY

November 14, 1968

The Arthur K. Salomon Lecture Series

The Arthur K. Salomon Lecture Series, established by a grant from the partners of Salomon Brothers & Hutzler in memory of a founding partner of the firm, is one of the diversified services provided by the Graduate School of Business Administration of New York University. In these meetings, distinguished scholars and men of national and international repute have shared their experiences, their wisdom and their leadership in the examination of crucial economic and financial problems of the day.

Previous Arthur K. Salomon lecturers:

February 1963

PER JACOBSSON
Chairman of the Executive Board and Managing Director
International Monetary Fund

"The Role of Money in a Dynamic Economy"

November 1963

ALLAN SPROUL
President
Federal Reserve Bank of New York 1941–1956

"Money Will Not Manage Itself"

November 1964

RUDOLPH A. PETERSON
President
Bank of America National Trust and Savings Association

"Debt in a New Environment"

November 1965

JOHN KENNETH GALBRAITH
Paul F. Warburg Professor of Economics
Harvard University

"Economic Policy Since 1945: The Nature of Success"

November 1966

THE RIGHT HONORABLE
THE EARL OF CROMER, M.B.E.
Formerly Governor of the Bank of England
"The International Capital Markets"

December 1967

PIERRE-PAUL SCHWEITZER
Managing Director

International Monetary Fund

"The New Arrangements to Supplement
World Reserves and Their Implications
For the Developing Countries"

Is Monetary Policy Being Oversold?

WALTER W. HELLER

My intent today is neither to praise nor to bury that towering iconoclast Milton Friedman, for to praise him and his works would absorb far too much of my limited time, and to bury him is, in a word, impossible.

Also, a word about the title, "Is Monetary Policy Being Oversold?" You should keep in mind that a speech title, like a biblical text, is a point of departure—and depart from it I shall. In one sense, in striving for symmetry with Milton's title, I may have made it too broad. It might better have read "Is Money Supply Being Oversold?" But since the twin topics under review are really fiscal versus monetary policy and discretionary versus automated policy, this title may be too narrow. In this sense, it might better have read "The Future of Discretionary Fiscal—and Monetary—Policy."

At the outset, let's clarify what is and what isn't at issue in today's discussion of fiscal-monetary policy, both inside and outside this hall. When we do this, I'm afraid that the lines may not be drawn quite as sharply as the journalists, who love a fight and drama, would have us believe with their headlines like "Is Keynes Defunct?" But have no fear. There will be plenty of grist for the mill of today's dialogue!

The issue is *not* whether money matters—we all grant that—but whether *only* money matters, as some Friedman-ites, or perhaps I should say Friedmanics, would put it. Or really, whether only money matters *much,* which is what I understand Milton Friedman to say—he is more reasonable than many of the Friedmanites.

It's important in this connection, too, to make clear that the economic policy of the 1960's, the "new economics" if you will, assigns an important role to *both* fiscal and mone-tary policy. Indeed, the appropriate mix of policies has often been the cornerstone of the argument: It was, for example, early in the 60's, when we feared that tight money might stunt recovery, might thwart the expansionary impact of the 1962–64 income tax cuts. It was again, in 1966, when in strongly urging a tax increase, we put heavy emphasis on avoiding the ill effects of imposing too much of the burden of restraint on Federal Reserve policy. It was once again, in 1967–68, when we sought the surtax in considerable part to insure against a repetition of the monetary crunch of 1966. And it will be in the future, when full employment surpluses in the federal budget may be the only defensible way to buy the monetary ease that commitment to rapid economic growth implies. In short, to anyone who might fear that the "new economics" is all fiscal policy, the record offers evidence, and the new economists offer assurance, that money *does* matter.

With that straw man removed, we can identify the real monetary issues with which the monetarists confront us:

First, should money supply be the sole or primary guide to Federal Reserve policy? Should it, at the very least, be ranged side by side with interest rates and credit availability in the Fed's affections? Second, should we rely on the Federal Reserve authorities to adapt monetary policy flexibly to changing economic events and to shifts in fiscal policy, or should we instead not only enthrone money supply but encase it in a rigid formula specifying a fixed increase of 3, 4, or 5 per cent a year? In other words, should we adopt the Friedman rule and replace Bill Martin at the Fed with an exponential curve—or would we simply be throwing him one?

Again, in the fiscal field, the issue is not *whether* fiscal policy matters—even some monetarists, perhaps in unguarded moments, have urged budget cuts or tax changes for stabilization reasons. The issues are *how much* it matters, and how heavily we can lean on discretionary changes in taxes and budgets to maintain steady economic growth in a dynamic economy: Is the close correlation of activist fiscal policy and strong expansion—which has brought our economy into the narrow band around full employment—a matter of accident or causation? Does a fair balancing of the successes and shortcomings of active fiscal policy suggest (a) that we should now take refuge in rigid fiscal rules like the lock-stop tax cuts espoused by Barry Goldwater and Milton Friedman, or rather (b) that we need to modify our fiscal institutions—especially our procedures for cutting or boosting taxes—to step up their speed and precision, especially in dealing with inflation?

Pervading these operational issues is a basic question of targets, as yet not answered in any conclusive way by either analysis or evidence. Should the target be, as the Phillips-curve analysis suggests, somewhat less unemployment in exchange for somewhat more price creep? Or is this trade-off illusory, as the adherents of the classical real-wage doctrine are now reasserting? To hark back to words and men of the past—Is a little inflation like a little pregnancy? Or was Sumner Slichter prophetic when he said that if we wanted to live with steady full employment and brisk growth, we also had to—and could—live with a little chronic inflation, with a price creep of 2 per cent or so a year?

Summing up the key operational issues, they are: Should money be king? Is fiscal policy worth its salt? Should flexible man yield to rigid rules? You will note that I purposely cast these issues in a show-me form to put both the monetarists and the new economists on their mettle.

Let me review with you the factors that say "stop, look, and listen" before embracing the triple doctrine that only money matters much; that control of the money supply is the key to economic stability; and that a rigid fixed-throttle expansion of 4 or 5 per cent a year is the only safe policy prescription in a world of alleged economic ignorance and human weakness and folly.

One should note in passing that Professor Friedman's findings and conclusions fit into a steady process of rescuing monetary policy from the limbo into which it was put by the interest-rate peg of World War II and the late 40's— a rescue effected by the Monetary Accord of 1951 and by the subsequent steady expansion of its scope. This has been a healthy renaissance. But having been resurrected from the debilitating rate peg of the 1940's, does monetary policy now face the threat of a new peg, Milton's money-supply peg, in the years ahead? Is it doomed to go from cradle to grave in twenty years?

I exaggerate, of course, for emphasis. President Nixon,

for example, has been reported as saying that he doesn't buy the fixed-throttle formula. At the same time, he has reportedly suggested that he intends to put more emphasis on money supply. So this is a particularly apt juncture for a close look at the monetarists' doctrine.

Now, turning to doubts, unresolved questions, and unconvincing evidence, I group these into eight conditions that must be satisfied—if not completely, at least more convincingly than they have been to date—before we can even consider giving money supply sovereignty, or dominance, or greater prominence in economic policy. These conditions center on such questions as: Which money-supply indicator do you believe? Can one read enough from money supply without weighing also shifts in demand and interest rates —that is, don't both quantity *and* price of money count? Don't observed variations in monetary time lags and velocity cast serious doubt on any simple relation between money supply and GNP? Can a rigid monetary rule find happiness in a world beset with rigidities and rather limited adjustment capabilities? That is, is the rigid Friedman rule perhaps a formula made in heaven, that will work only in heaven?

I claim no originality in my catalogue of doubts. My debt to people like James Tobin, John Kareken, Lyle Gramley, and others, whose painstaking research and analysis I draw on, is virtually complete.[1]

The first condition is this: the monetarists must make up their minds which money-supply variable they want us to accept as our guiding star—M_1, the narrow money supply, just currency and bank deposits; M_2, adding time deposits; or perhaps some other measure like the "monetary base?" And when will the monetarists decide? Perhaps Milton Friedman has decided; but if he has, his disciples do not seem to have gotten the word.

Let me give you an example. Last spring, M_1 (the money stock) was all the rage. It spurted for four months in a row, from April through July. But when that slowed down, most of the alarmists switched horses to M_2 (money plus time deposits), which quite conveniently began rising sharply in July. And listen to the latest release from the St. Louis Federal Reserve Bank—the unofficial statistical arm of the Chicago School—which very carefully throws a sop to all sides: "Monetary expansion since July has decelerated as measured by the money stock, accelerated as measured by money plus time deposits, and remained at about an unchanged rate as measured by the monetary base. As a result, questions arise as to which monetary aggregate may be currently most meaningful in indicating monetary influence on economic activity." [2] Precisely.

It doesn't seem too much to ask that this confusion be resolved in some satisfactory way before putting great faith in money supply as our key policy variable.

Second, I would feel more sympathetic to the money-supply doctrine if it were not so one-track-minded about money stock—measured any way you wish—as the *only* financial variable with any informational content for policy purposes.

As Gramley has noted, for example, if we look at money stock alone for 1948, it would indicate the tightest money in the post-war period.[3] Yet, the rate on Treasury bills was 1 per cent, and on high-grade corporates 2¾ per cent. (That *does* sound like ancient history.) But isn't it curious that we had tight money by the money-supply standard side by side with 1, 2, and 3 percent interest rates? We were swamped with liquidity—so interest rates do seem to have been telling us something very important.

Or, if we look at 1967 *only* in terms of the money stock, it would appear as the easiest-money year since World War II. M_1 was up 6 per cent, M_2 was up 12 per cent. Yet there was a very sharp rise in interest rates. Why? Probably because of a big shift in liquidity preference as corporations strove to build up their protective liquidity cushions after their harrowing experience the previous year—their monetary dehydration in the credit crunch of 1966. Again, the behavior of interest rates is vital to proper interpretation of monetary developments and guidance of monetary policy. Interest rates are endogenous variables and cannot be used alone—but neither can money stock. Either interest rates or money stock, used alone, could seriously mislead us.

I really don't understand how the scarcity of any commodity can be gauged without referring to its price—or, more specifically, how the scarcity of money can be gauged without referring to interest rates. It may, strictly speaking, be wrong to identify any market interest rate as the price of money. In the U. S., no interest is paid either on demand deposits or on currency. But this is quibbling. The point is that a change in the demand for money relative to the supply, or a change in the supply relative to demand, results generally in a change in interest rates.[4] To insist that the behavior of the price of money (interest rates) conveys no information about its scarcity is, as Tobin has noted, an "odd heresy."

Third, given the fluctuations in money velocity, that supposedly inexorable link between money and economic activity has yet to be established. We should not forget this, however sweet the siren song of the monetarists may sound. We should not forget the revealing passage from that monumental Friedman-Schwartz volume, *A Monetary History of the United States,* that makes my point:

. . . the observed year-to-year change in velocity was
less than 10 per cent in 78 out of 91 year-to-year changes
from 1869, when our velocity figures start, to 1960. Of
the 13 larger changes, more than half came during
either the Great Contraction or the two world wars,
and the largest change was 17 per cent. Expressed as
a percentage of a secular trend, velocity was within the
range of 90 to 110 in 53 years, 85 to 115 in 66 years.
of the remaining 26 years, 12 were during the first 15
years, for which the income figures are seriously defec-
tive, and 17 during the Great Contraction and the two
wars.[5]

Clearly, velocity has varied over time—some might say
"greatly," others "moderately." Let me sidestep a bit and
say, for purposes of this discussion, "significantly." For I
would remind you that the income velocity of money rose
roughly 28 per cent during the 1960–68 period. Had velocity
been the same in 1968 as it was in 1960, nominal GNP
would have been not some $860 billion, but only $675
billion.

What Friedman and Schwartz report, then, about the
behavior of velocity suggests that there are other factors
—strangely, such fiscal actions as tax cuts or budget changes
come to mind—that influence the level of economic activity.
Velocity has changed, as it were, to accommodate these
other influences and will go on doing so, I have no doubt,
in the future.

The observed changes in velocity underscore the broader
point I was hinting at a moment ago: The Friedman-
Schwartz study did not find anything like a near-perfect
correlation—a rigid link—between money and economic
activity. And such correlation as they did find was based
on complex and often quite arbitrary adjustments of their

raw data. It was Tobin who noted that the regularities which Professor Friedman claims to have detected in his data are quite esoteric!

This reminds us again that Friedman and Schwartz use an incomplete model of the U. S. economy in testing the potency of money supply. Perhaps, had they used a more complete model, they might have found not only less potency but greater precision in the effects of changes in the money supply (and hence, by the way, less need for a rigid monetary rule). Before succumbing to their massive and impressive array of data, observers in general and policy makers in particular should be clear that the Friedman-Schwartz findings neither prove that "only money matters much" nor disprove that fiscal policy matters a great deal.[6]

Fourth, it would help us if the monetarists could narrow the range on *when* money matters. How long *are* the lags that have to be taken into account in managing monetary policy? Here, I quote from Professor Friedman's tour de force, *A Program for Monetary Stability:*

> In the National Bureau study on which I have been collaborating with Mrs. Schwartz we found that, on the average of 18 cycles, peaks in the rate of change in the stock of money tend to precede peaks in general business by about 16 months and troughs in the rate of change in the stock of money to precede troughs in general business by about 12 months. . . . For individual cycles, the recorded lag has varied between 6 and 29 months at peaks and between 4 and 22 months at troughs.[7]

So the Friedman-Schwartz study found a long average lag, and just as important it would seem, a highly variable lag. But why this considerable variance? No doubt there are sev-

eral possible answers. But again, the most natural one is
that the level of economic activity, or total demand for the
nation's output, is influenced by variables other than the
stock of money—possibly even by tax rates and federal
spending and transfer payments!

Suppose I told you that I had checked and found that in
repeated trials, it required from 100 to 300 feet for a car
going so and so many miles an hour to stop. That is quite
a range. But would you be surprised? I think not. You would
simply remind me that the distance it takes a car to stop
depends, among other things, on the condition of the road
surface. If I had allowed for the condition of the road surface, I would not have ended up with such a wide range
of stopping distances.

Just so. If Professor Friedman and Mrs. Schwartz had
taken account of other variables that influence total demand,
or if they had estimated the lag of monetary policy using a
complete model of the U. S. economy, they would not have
found the lag of monetary policy to be quite so variable.
Again, then, one correctly infers that their findings are quite
consistent with fiscal policy mattering, and mattering a great
deal. Nor is it necessarily relevant, as some have suggested,
that in the middle of the nineteenth century, the government
sector was relatively small. Variables other than changes in
tax rates and government expenditures and transfers can
"distort" the money-income lag.

Professor Friedman has also used this finding of (a) a
long average lag and (b) a highly variable lag in support
of his plea for steady growth of the money supply. With so
long an average lag, the argument goes, forecasters are help-
less; they cannot see twelve or fifteen months into the future
with any accuracy. And even if they could, they would be
at a loss to know how far ahead to appraise the economic

outlook. But I doubt that he can properly draw this inference from his finding of a long and highly variable lag.

It seems to me misleading to estimate a discreet lag as the Friedman-Schwartz team did. It's reasonable to suppose, given the research findings of other investigators, that the effect of a change in monetary policy cumulates through time. To begin, there's a slight effect; and as time passes, the effect becomes more pronounced. But insofar as the feasibility of discretionary monetary policy is at issue, what matters *most* is whether there is some near-term effect. If there is, then the Federal Reserve can influence the economy one quarter or two quarters from now. That there are subsequent, more pronounced, effects is not the key question. These subsequent effects get caught, as it were, in subsequent forecasts of the economic outlook, and current policy is adjusted accordingly. At least this is what happens in a non-Friedmanic world where one enjoys the benefits of discretionary policy changes.

Lest I leave any doubt about what I infer from this: if there is a near-immediate effect from a change in policy, then discretionary monetary policy does not impose an unbearable burden on forecasters. For six or nine months ahead, they can do reasonably well. But given the too-discreet way Friedman-Schwartz went about estimating the lag of monetary policy, I see no way of determining the shape of the monetary policy lag. Until they know more about the shape of this lag, I don't see how they can insist on a monetary rule.

Fifth, I'd be happier if only I knew which of the two Friedmans to believe. Should it be the Friedman we have had in focus here—the Friedman of the close causal relationship between money supply and income, who sees changes in money balances worked off gradually, with long lags before interest rates, prices of financial and physical assets, and, eventually, investment and consumption spending are affected? Or should it be the Friedman of the "permanent-income hypothesis," who sees the demand for money as quite unresponsive to changes in current income (since current income has only a fractional weight in permanent income), with the implied result that the monetary multiplier is very large in the short run, that there is an immediate and strong response to a change in the money stock? As Tobin has noted, he can't have it both ways. But which is it to be?

Sixth, if Milton's policy prescription were made in a frictionless Friedmanesque world without price, wage, and exchange rigidities—a world of his own making—it would be more admissible. But in the imperfect world in which we actually operate, beset by all sorts of rigidities, the introduction of his fixed-throttle money-supply rule might, in fact, be destabilizing. Or it could condemn us to long periods of economic slack or inflation as the slow adjustment processes in wages and prices, given strong market power, delayed the economy's reaction to the monetary rule while policy makers stood helplessly by.

A seventh and closely related concern is that locking the money supply into a rigid rule would jeopardize the U. S. international position. It's quite clear that capital flows are interest-rate sensitive. Indeed, capital flows induced by interest-rate changes can increase alarmingly when speculators take over. Under the Friedman rule, market interest rates would be whatever they turned out to be. It would be beyond the pale for the Fed to adjust interest rates for balance-of-payments adjustment purposes. Nor is it clear that by operating in the market for forward exchange (which in any event Milton would presumably oppose) the system could altogether neutralize changes in domestic market rates.

Milton has heard all of this before, and he always has an answer—flexible exchange rates. Parenthetically, I fully understand that it's much easier to debate Milton in absentia than in person! Yet, suffice it to note that however vital they are to the workings of his money-supply peg, floating exchange rates are not just around the corner.

As my heavenly reference suggested, then, in the real world, Milton and the monetarists are quite safe. Their theory and policy prescriptions won't be put to the test of application, so there will be no chance to disprove them.

Eighth, and finally, if the monetarists showed some small willingness to recognize the impact of fiscal policy—which has played such a large role in the policy thinking and action underlying the great expansion of the 1960's—one might be a little more sympathetic to their views. This point is, I must admit, not so much a condition as a plea for symmetry. The "new economists," having already given important and increasing weight to monetary factors in their policy models, are still waiting for signs that the monetarists will admit fiscal factors to theirs.

The 1964 tax cut pointedly illustrates what I mean. While the "new economists" fully recognize the important role monetary policy played in facilitating the success of the tax cut, the monetarists go to elaborate lengths to "prove" that the tax cut—which came close to removing a $13 billion full-employment surplus that was overburdening and retarding the economy—had nothing to do with the 1964–65 expansion. Money-supply growth did it all. Apparently, we were just playing fiscal tiddlywinks in Washington.

It seems to me that the cause of balanced analysis and rational policy would be served by redirecting some of the brilliance of Friedman and his followers from (a) single-mindedly devotion to the money-supply thesis and unceasing efforts to discredit fiscal policy and indeed all discretionary policy to (b) joint efforts to develop a more complete and satisfactory model of how the real world works; ascertain why it is working far better today than it did before active and conscious fiscal-monetary policy came into play; and determine how such policy can be improved to make it work even better in the future.

In a related asymmetry, as I've already suggested in passing, some Friedmanites fail to recognize that if fiscal policy actions like the 1964 tax cut can do no good, then fiscal policy actions like the big budget increases and deficits associated with Vietnam can also do no harm. Again, they should recognize that they can't have it both ways.

Now, one could lengthen and elaborate this list. But enough—let's just round it off this way: if Milton Friedman were saying that (as part of an active discretionary policy) we had better keep a closer eye on that important variable, money supply, in one or more of its several incarnations —I would say well and good, by all means. If the manifold doubts can be reasonably resolved, let's remedy any neglect or underemphasis of money supply as a policy indicator relative to interest rates, free reserves, and the like. But let's not lock the steering gear into place, knowing full well of the twists and turns in the road ahead. That's an invitation to chaos.

Suppose for a moment that a conservative president, heeding—as indeed the Republican candidate seemed to in 1964 —the counsel of the monetarists, (a) persuaded the Federal Reserve Board to set monetary policy on a rigid path of 4 or 5 per cent annual increases in monetary supply, and (b) persuaded the Congress to freeze tax policy into a pattern of once-a-year income tax cuts as Senator Goldwater proposed in '64 and as Arthur Burns seemed to be suggesting last week.

With the controls thus locked into place—I started to say, "with the controls thus on automatic pilot," but that's the wrong figure of speech because the automatic pilot adjusts for changes in the wind and other atmospheric conditions —one can imagine what would happen when the economy encountered the turbulence of recession with its downdrafts in jobs, profits, and incomes. How long could Richard Nixon, for example, stand idly by and deny himself and the country the proven tonic of tax cuts, spending speedups, and easier money? Economic common sense and political sagacity—and he has both—would soon win out, I am sure, over the rigid and static rules that so ill befit an ever changing and dynamic economy. So as a practical matter, I don't expect the country to fall into the trap of lockstep economics in the Nixon Administration or any other administration of the foreseeable future. I fully expect the new Administration to practice active discretionary fiscal and monetary policy.

This may put me, I realize, in the strange position of defending the Nixon Administration against one of its own advisors. But, as the lady psychiatrist at a convention of psychiatrists said to herself when she was about to slap a male colleague sitting next to her who was taking certain liberties—"Why should I? That's *his* problem!"

Having paid my debt to the title of this talk, let me turn now to the more positive side of my assignment. Two important tasks remain. The first is to remind you of the potency and effectiveness of fiscal policy. The second is to restate the case for continued and expanded use of discretionary, man-made policy in preference to rigid monetary and fiscal rules.

Again, we need to stop, look, and listen lest we let simplistic or captious criticism operate to deny us the benefits of past experience and thwart the promise of future discretionary action on the monetary and fiscal fronts.

Perhaps the best way to begin is to move back from a day-by-day or month-by-month perspective to ask this broad question: What has been the course of the American economy during the postwar period of an increasingly active and self-conscious fiscal-monetary policy for economic stabilization? Or, for that matter, let's broaden it: what has been the course of the world's advanced industrial economies during this period? The correlation is unmistakable: the more active, informed, and self-conscious fiscal and monetary policies have become, by and large, the more fully employed and stable the affected economies have become. Casual empiricism? Perhaps—yet a powerful and persuasive observation.

Witness the conclusion of the two-and-a-half–year study for the OECD by a group of fiscal experts from eight industrial countries:

> The postwar economic performance of most Western countries in respect of employment, production and growth has been vastly superior to that of the pre-war years. This, in our view, has not been accidental. Governments have increasingly accepted responsibility for the promotion and maintenance of high employment and steady economic growth. The more conscious use of economic policies has undoubtedly played a crucial role in the better performance achieved—an achievement which, from the point of view of the ultimate social objectives of policy, is of paramount importance.[8]

Perhaps an even more telling testament to the effectiveness of active modern stabilization-policy is the change in private investment thinking and planning not only in the financial sense of sustained confidence in the future of corporate earnings and stock market values, even in the face of temporary slowdowns in the economy—but more important, in the physical sense of sustained high levels of plant and equipment investment which seem to be replacing the sickening swings that used to be the order of the day.

Why? In good part, I take it to be the result of a constantly deepening conviction in the business and financial community that alert and active fiscal-monetary policy will keep the economy operating at a higher proportion of its potential in the future than in the past; that beyond short and temporary slowdowns, or perhaps even a recession—that's not ruled out in this vast and dynamic economy of ours—lies the prospect of sustained growth in that narrow band around full employment.

Going beyond these general observations, we have to look at specific economic experience for cause-and-effect sequences that demonstrate the potency of fiscal policy. Don't expect me to assert that we have proof, absolute proof, of this causal sequence. But quibbles about exact timing aside, the potency of fiscal policy—both good and bad—has been demonstrated time and again in the past couple of decades.

First, the contrast between the fiscal record and economic consequences of the Vietnam and Korean wars is particularly instructive. In 1950–51, three tax bills that, in today's GNP terms, boosted taxes by $35-$40 billion paved the way for some four years of price stability (after an initial spurt that ended by mid–1951) without resort to excessively tight money. In 1966–68, Vietnam escalation coupled with initial Presidential hesitation to ask for a tax boost and later Congressional delay in enacting one led to the opposite result: growing deficits and an accelerating inflation (interrupted only by the late–1966 and early–1967 slowdown after the monetary brakes were slammed on and some fiscal restraints were imposed).

Second, in 1959–60, a growing full-employment surplus which reached a level of more than $10 billion, reinforced by rising interest rates, pushed the economy back into recession after only twenty-five months of expansion. Here we have another prime example of the penalty for failure to act, a penalty that was widely predicted by economists, both liberal and conservative, outside the Eisenhower Administration.

Third, the great expansion of the 1960's is another case in point. Deliberate tax cuts and both deliberate and non-deliberate expenditure increases played the key role in the thinking of economic policy makers, in official forecasts of changes in the level of economic activity, and in the actual GNP developments that materialized. And when urgently-recommended steps to increase taxes were not taken, the predicted consequences of overheating and inflation and undue burdens on monetary policy were amply and painfully borne out. Both in the breach and in the observance, fiscal policy demonstrated its potency during the 1960's.

The capstone of postwar policy for putting the U. S. economy more or less permanently into the full-employment orbit was, of course, the great tax cut of 1964. Coupled with the 1962 tax measures to stimulate investment, it reduced both individual and corporate income tax liabilities by one fifth. As for its economic impact: (1) as already noted, it virtually cleared away the last great obstacle to full employment, that $12 to $13 billion full-employment surplus under whose crushing weight we were simply unable to struggle to full employment. Put more starkly, to get full employment without the tax cut would have required $12 to $13 billion of additional private investment to offset a like amount of government saving. (2) Monetary policy played an important supporting role in accommodating the expansionary thrust of the tax cut. The Fed did not permit rising interest rates or tightening credit to choke off its stimulative impact. (3) The pace of economic advance accelerated as expected. By mid–1965, just before Vietnam escalation undid us, the old peacetime record for duration of U.S. expansions, fifty-one months, toppled, and rapidly expanding employment had brought the jobless rate to 4½ per cent. (4) In this process, the tax cut cleared away many of the obstacles of economic myth and misunderstanding that had long blocked the path to full use of our monetary and fiscal tools.

As we near a five-year perspective on the tax cut, we begin to see it as an economic watershed, the end of one era and the beginning of another. It ended an era in which the country felt it could afford to tolerate—or, given the available economic tools and understanding, *needed* to tolerate—chronic unemployment and underutilization of its resources (which characterized eight of the ten years between 1955 and 1965). It ushered in a new era in which the avowed and active use of tax, budget, and monetary instruments would keep the economy operating in the vicinity of full employment, with all the pleasures and pains that the management of prosperity involves (a state that most of our partners in the industrial world have enjoyed and suffered for some time).

But great as its contribution was in removing barriers to full employment and public understanding—and in bearing out the analysis and forecasts in which the tax cut was anchored—it has relatively little to offer us in the management of policy in the narrow band (aside from serving as further confirming evidence on such economic relationships as those reflected in the multiplier). Why ?

Primarily, because the requirement today is for much more nimble and faster action than a chronically or repeatedly underemployed economy typically requires. It was a semantic misfortune that this requirement was put in terms of "fine tuning" in 1967. What we were referring to was simply the need to shift from stimulus to restraint at about mid-year. But given the glee with which the term is being attacked—the critics imply that it means constant fiddling with the fiscal-monetary dials—I'm afraid that "fine tuning" is about to join "the Puritan ethic" in the gallery of gaffes in economic-policy semantics.

Yet, lampooning aside, the term "fine tuning" brings an important issue into focus. For policy tolerances become much narrower in the high-employment economic zone. Fiscal and monetary actions must not only pack a punch, but that punch has to be delivered with greater speed and precision—and with greater courage as well, since inflation is so often the foe in a high-employment, high-growth economy.

That throws the issue of man versus rules, discretion versus automaticity, into bold relief. The monetarists tell the policy maker, in effect, "Don't do something, just stand there." They doubt that we have the economic wisdom, the strength of character, and the institutional capability to operate a successful discretionary policy. In their view, rigid rules would outperform mortal man.

Time and space do not permit a full review here of the case for discretionary and flexible policy.[9] Quite apart from the basic flaw in the concept of living by rules alone—namely, that there is no escape from discretion, if only in setting the rules and changing them from time to time—I have already suggested a couple of practical defects. (1) In anything but a world of flexible price, cost, and exchange adjustments, fixed rates of change in the money stock and tax levels are more likely to be destabilizing than stabilizing. (2) It offends common sense to say that policy should (or would) deny itself the increasingly broad, prompt, and reliable current economic information available to us, let alone, the forecasts grounded in this growing fund of information and knowledge of economic relationships.

Yet, doubts about the limits of discretion persist. In terms of the economic policies of the 60's, they center on (a) the halting performance in dealing with Vietnam-induced inflation in the past three years; (b) the slow response of GNP to last June's tax hike and budget cutback; and (c) occasional errors in official economic forecasts. Close inspection of experience in all three cases offers, I submit, solid reasons for pushing ahead along the path of discretionary policy rather than taking refuge in rigid rules.

First, then, we turn to the lessons of 1966–68. The tendency is to say that we did so poorly in coping with inflation that it bodes ill for the future of discretionary and monetary policy. One can join the chorus of critics of 1966–68 policy without accepting the gloomy inference for the future. A more hopeful inference about our ability and will to cope with excess demand in the future can be drawn from the following facts:

(1) The Economic Advisers' diagnosis of the economy's ills was, in general, correct, and their prescription was apt. As President Johnson recently revealed, his advisers unanimously recommended a tax increase early in 1966 as part of their prescription for what ailed the economy. But Drs. Johnson and Mills were slow to fill the prescription and apply it to the patient. One might add that Dr. Ford and a few others on the other side of the aisle were even slower to accept the diagnosis and prescription.

(2) Some of the difficulties that plagued economic policy were *sui generis*. Can you imagine a repeat of the situation in the second half of 1965 when the Council of Economic Advisers and the Treasury—judging by the speeches of their top men—were not aware of the Pentagon's expenditure plans? Or a period when a block of expenditures as large as those for Vietnam were underestimated again and again to the point where one agency in Washington footnoted an "official" estimate of military expenditures as follows: "For internal use only, but dangerous if swallowed!"

(3) Just as we moved from fiscal fiction and fallacy to fiscal fact and understanding in the course of debate and action on the 1964 tax cut, so it seems to me we learned a great deal in the two-and-a-half–year hassle over the tax increase. The newspaper headline last spring, "Market Rallies on Hope of Tax Boost," is a case in point. Failure to act on taxes was, as predicted, so costly in terms of higher prices, higher interest rates, higher imports, and higher deficits, that the lesson for the future was inescapable. Never again, I should judge, would a President hesitate so long or a Congress sit idly by while inflation takes us by the throat as it did in 1966–68.

(4) Congress did, after all, pass the tax surcharge and the budget cutback. After that unconscionable and costly delay, it was still an act of political courage—coming as it did, just five months before a national election. And judging by the high ratio of incumbents who voted for the surtax in June and won reelection in November, it didn't involve nearly the political penalties that had been feared. That, too, is a good portent for the future.

(5) In the future, the fiscal fight against inflation can ordinarily be fought without resort to the grueling and gruesome process of wringing a tax increase out of Congress

For revenues from existing taxes (the surtax aside) will grow by some $15 billion a year, as an automatic by-product of growth in GNP. It should be a lot easier to exercise fiscal restraint by holding back some of this revenue bounty (i.e., by not declaring "fiscal dividends" through program increases or tax cuts) than it has been to ram a tax increase through a reluctant Congress.

Second, after the long executive and legislative lags on the 10 per cent surtax, how does the advocate of discretionary fiscal action deal with the lag in economic response to this measure after its enactment last June?

(1) By confessing that many, if not most, of us who make specific forecasts have a bit of egg on our face. We expected a cooling off of the economy to be well under way by now, but the overall advance in GNP seems to be holding up better than expected.

(2) By reminding you that the surcharge *is* doing some of the work expected of it, not just in the sense of "think of how much worse off we would be if we hadn't acted," but in the performance of retail sales, which peaked at $29 billion in August (after rising more than $2½ billion during 1968) and have not reached that level since; of real GNP, which forged ahead at an annual rate of nearly 6½ per cent in the first couple of quarters, slowed to 4.9 per cent in the third quarter, seems headed down to about 3½ per cent in the current quarter, and perhaps 1 to 2 per cent in the first couple of quarters next year.

(3) By noting that during the long delay in enacting the fiscal package, cost and price pressures became more intense, and inflationary expectations became more embedded in investment thinking, than most observers realized. Coupled with growing confidence in sustained expansion, this has lessened the risks associated with capital spending and

debt. Advances in plant and equipment spending, housing, and durable goods purchases have all exceeded expectations.

I should add that if the expected healthy easing of the economy does occur early next year, it won't provide any clear-cut decision after all on the relative impacts of fiscal and monetary policy. The recent slowdown in the growth of the money supply (at least in its M_1 version) deprives us of what might have been a reasonably clear-cut confrontation. What a sad day for those who had so eagerly awaited a test-tube experiment!

Finally, this brings us to the prickly area of economic forecasting. One of Milton Friedman's main charges against discretionary policy is that economic forecasting is a weak reed on which to lean in guiding policy action. The contrary view, which I hold, is that we cannot operate intelligent economic policies—public or private—without forecasts. We have to make the most reasonable forecast of the future and then be as nimble and flexible as possible in adjusting to unforeseen events and forces.

Official forecasters have, as you know, been leading a mighty exposed life ever since the beginning of President Kennedy's Administration, when we reversed previous practice by laying forecasts on the line publicly. I hope and assume that future administrations will not change this practice.

What's the right test to apply in judging whether forecasting can carry the burden that is required for discretionary policy? The right test, I submit, is not whether annual GNP forecasts are accurate to the nearest $5 or $10 billion, but whether they are sufficiently right in predicting the direction and intensity of change, first, to avoid *wrong* policy advice (for if they do no more than that, they have

already at least matched automatic, or lockstep, policy);
second, to lead to the *right* policy advice, if not every time,
at least a very high proportion of the time.

Now by that reasonable standard, I submit that official
forecasts since 1960 have fallen from grace for only four
brief periods: early 1962, when we thought the economy
was going to be a lot more exuberant than it turned out
to be, and we didn't switch our forecast until May of that
year; late 1965 and early 1966, when the economic force of
Vietnam was at best dimly perceived; the fall of 1966, when
economic softness crept up on us unawares and was not
recognized for about six weeks; the well known 1968 example we are still experiencing.

But the rest of the time, official economic forecasts have
correctly led the President's economic advisers to urge expansionary action from early 1961 to the first half of 1965;
to urge restrictive fiscal-monetary policy in 1966; to urge
a roller-coaster policy in 1967, consisting of (a) fiscal-
monetary ease early in the year to avert recession and
then (b) a call for the surtax after mid-year to help ward
off resurgent inflation; and to urge, with ever greater intensity, prompt enactment of the surtax in 1968.

That inevitably moves us from the alleged weakness of
forecasting to the weakness of the flesh. For what shall it
profit us if we can correctly forecast overheating and pre-
scribe the right policy medicine, but Wilbur Mills heedeth
us not? Or, as some other wit dimly suggested, that the tax
Mills grind exceeding fine, or may even grind to a halt?

That is a none-too-subtle way of bringing me to the point
that we need to bend every effort to make fiscal policy—and
particularly tax policy—more responsive and flexible. Indeed, if tax rates can be adjusted quickly and flexibly to
ebbs and flows of aggregate demand, the penalties for

errors in forecasting would be correspondingly reduced. We must find a way to make tax rates more adaptable to economic circumstances, either by granting the President stand-by power to make temporary cuts and increases in the income tax (subject to Congressional veto); or by setting up speedier Congressional procedures to respond to Presidential requests for quick tax changes to head off recession or inflation; or by developing the executive practice (proposed by a Nixon task force) under which the President would, as part of his budget message each January, propose a positive or negative income surtax (for stabilization purposes).

In winding up these comments, let me say that just as the monetarists have a great deal still to clarify, establish, and correct before they can lay claim to an only-money-matters-much economic policy, so the economic activists—I won't say "fiscalists," because economic activism implies a balanced policy of fiscal and monetary discretion—still have a great deal to learn about operating in the narrow band around full employment; a great deal more to do in improving forecasting; and important worlds to conquer in speeding up the executive and legislative processes and developing the skills to manage the fiscal dividend so as not to let it retard normal expansion, and yet, when the economy overheats, to let it become a welcome fiscal drag.

In my comments today, I referred to the brilliance of the Chicago School. I should also comment on their great consistency over the years. The rest of us—responding to new analysis and evidence, observing basic changes in the economy, and conditioned (or perhaps "burned") by experience and on-the-job training—adapt and modify our views from time to time on such key issues as (a) the role and desirability of government tax incentives for investments; (b) the independence of the Fed; (c) the proper mix of tax cuts, government budget increases, and tax sharing; and (d) yes, even the relative roles of fiscal and monetary policy. In short, we have yet to encounter the revealed and immutable truth.

But the Chicago school just goes rolling along. Miraculously, all the evidence—I really mean, all the admissible evidence—strengthens their conviction, held for decades, that to err is human, and to live by rules is divine. In spite of vast improvements in the promptness, breadth, and accuracy of economic statistics, in spite of important advances in forecasting techniques and performance, in spite of vast strides in public understanding and acceptance of positive economic policy, in spite of encouraging signs of greater responsiveness of executive and legislative officials to informed economic policy advice, the Chicago School still adheres to the proposition that we should put our trust in stable formulas, not in unstable men and institutions.

That's a bit of a caricature, but only a bit. The monetarists have taught us much. We are far richer for their analyses and painstaking research. But we would be far poorer, I believe, for following their policy prescription. It is high time that they stop trying to establish a single variable—money supply—as all-powerful, or nearly so, and stop striving to disestablish another variable—fiscal policy—as impotent, or nearly so. The path to progress in economic policy lies, instead, in a mutual undertaking to work out the best possible combination of fiscal, monetary, and wage-price policies—coupled with measures to speed the rise in productivity—for reconciling sustained high employment with reasonable price stability.

Has Fiscal Policy
Been Oversold?

MILTON FRIEDMAN

I am delighted to share the platform with Walter Heller today. Walter and I have been friends for a long time, and disagreement is part of the spice of friendship. I am delighted also to agree with him on some of the rules of today's game: for example, that we are not engaging in a debate, but are simply evaluating the substantive issues of monetary and fiscal policy, and, more seriously, that our discussion has no political element whatsoever because I, at least, shall speak not for any mythical Chicago School, not for any administration or candidate, but for myself. It is one of the great virtues and one of the great advantages of being a professor at a university, which those among you who are so unfortunate as to have to earn your living in the business world do not share, that we can be completely independent and irresponsible, and say what we really believe.

Let me start by saying that Walter has set up something of a straw man when he says that the issue is not whether money matters, but whether only money matters. I have never myself been able to accept that way of putting the issue. I do not think that it is a meaningful statement. Only money matters for what? If you want to have happiness in your home, the kind of money that matters is not the kind we're talking about now. It isn't Federal Reserve policy; it's income that matters.

More generally, there are many, many different things that matter for many, many different purposes. The key source of misunderstanding about the issue of monetary policy, in my opinion, has been the failure to distinguish clearly what it is that money matters for. What I and those who share my views have emphasized is that the quantity of money is extremely important for nominal magnitudes, for nominal income, for the level of income in dollars—important for what happens to prices. It is not important at all, or, if that's perhaps an exaggeration, not very important, for what happens to real output over the long period.

I have been increasingly impressed that much of the disagreement about this issue stems from the fact that an important element in the Keynesian revolution in economics was the notion that prices are an institutional datum determined outside the system. Once you take that view, once you say that prices are somehow determined elsewhere, then the distinction between nominal magnitudes and real magnitudes disappears. The distinction between magnitudes in dollars and magnitudes in terms of goods and services is no longer important.

That is why the qualifications we have always attached to our statements about the importance of money tend to be overlooked. We have always stressed that money matters a great deal for the development of nominal magnitudes, but not over the long run for real magnitudes. That qualification has tended to be dropped and a straw man has been set up to the effect that we say that money is the only thing that matters for the development of the economy. That's an absurd position, of course, and one that I have never held. The real wealth of a society depends much more on the kind of institutional structure it has, on the abilities, initiative, driving force of its people, on investment potentialities, on technology—on all of those things. That's what really matters from the point of view of the level of output. But, how many dollars will that be valued at? When you ask that question, that's where money matters.

Let me turn more directly to the topics assigned for this session. Is fiscal policy being oversold? Is monetary policy being oversold? I want to stress that my answer is yes to both of those questions. I believe monetary policy is being oversold; I believe fiscal policy is being oversold. What I believe is that fine tuning has been oversold. And this is not a new conclusion. I am delighted to attest to the correctness of Walter's statement that many of our views have not changed over time. It so happens that the facts haven't been inconsistent with them, and, therefore, we haven't had to change them over time.

Just this past week I was reading proof on a collection of technical essays of mine written much earlier that is going to appear next year (1969), and I came across a paper I gave to the Joint Economic Committee in 1958. I would like to quote from that paper, written ten years ago, some sentences which expressed my view at that time, and which still express my view today, on the issue of fine tuning, rather than on the separate issues of monetary and fiscal policy.

I said: "A steady rate of growth in the money supply will not mean perfect stability even though it would prevent the kind of wide fluctuations that we have experienced from time to time in the past. It is tempting to try to go farther and to use monetary changes to offset other factors making for expansion and contraction. . . . The available evidence . . . casts grave doubts on the possibility of producing any fine adjustments in economic activity by fine adjustments in monetary policy—at least in the present state of knowledge. . . . There are thus serious limitations to the possibility of a discretionary monetary policy and much danger that such a policy may make matters worse rather than better."

I went on: "To avoid misunderstanding, it should be emphasized that the problems just discussed are in no way peculiar to monetary policy. . . . The basic difficulties and limitations of monetary policy apply with equal force to fiscal policy."

And then I went on, "Political pressures to 'do something' in the face of either relatively mild price rises or relatively mild price and employment declines are clearly very strong indeed in the existing state of public attitudes. The main moral to be drawn from the two preceding points is that yielding to these pressures may frequently do more harm than good. There is a saying that the best is often the enemy of the good, which seems highly relevant. The goal of an extremely high degree of economic stability is certainly a splendid one. Our ability to attain it, however, is limited; we can surely avoid extreme fluctuations; we do not know enough to avoid minor fluctuations; the attempt to do more than we can will itself be a disturbance that may increase rather than reduce instability. But like all such injunctions, this one too must be taken in moderation. It is a plea for a sense of perspective and balance, not for irresponsibility in the face of major problems or for failure to correct past mistakes." [1]

Well, that was a view that I expressed ten years ago, and I do not believe that the evidence of the past ten years gives the lie to that view. I think that the evidence of the past ten years rather reinforces it, rather shows the difficulties of trying to engage in a very fine tuning of economic policy. I would emphasize today even more than I did then my qualifications with respect to monetary policy because thanks fundamentally, I think, to the difficulties that have been experienced with fiscal policy and to the experience of other countries, there has been an enormous shift in opinion.

Walter says we all know that money matters; it's only a question of whether it matters very much. His saying that is, in itself, evidence of the shift in opinion. Before coming up here today I reread the reports of the Council of Economic Advisers that were published when he was chairman of the Council. [2] I do not believe that anybody can read those reports and come out with the conclusion that they say that money matters significantly. While there was some attention paid to money in those reports, it was very limited.

There has been a tremendous change in opinion on this subject since then. And I am afraid that change may go too far. I share very much the doubts that Walter expressed about the closeness of the monetary relations. There is a very good relation on the average. But the relation is not close enough, it is not precise enough, so that you can, with enormous confidence, predict from the changes in the money supply in one quarter precisely what's going to happen in the next quarter or two quarters later.

Indeed, that's the major reason why I'm in favor of a rule. If I thought I could predict precisely, well then, to go back to the statement I quoted from, I would be prepared to make fine adjustments to offset other forces making for change. It's precisely because we don't know how to predict precisely that you cannot in fact use monetary policy effectively for this purpose. So I emphasize that my basic view is that what has been oversold is the notion of fine tuning.

Yet, fiscal policy has, in my view, been oversold in a very different and more basic sense than monetary policy—to turn to the main subject assigned to me. I believe that the rate of change of the money supply by itself—and I'm going to come back to those two words "by itself"—has a very important effect on nominal income and prices in the long run. It has a very important effect on fluctuations in nominal and real income in the short run. That's my basic conclusion about changes in the stock of money.

Now let's turn to fiscal policy. I believe that the state of the government budget matters; matters a great deal—for some things. The state of the government budget determines what fraction of the nation's income is spent through the government and what fraction is spent by individuals privately. The state of the government budget determines what the level of our taxes is, how much of our income we turn over to the government. The state of the government budget has a considerable effect on interest rates. If the federal government runs a large deficit, that means the government has to borrow in the market, which raises the demand for loanable funds and so tends to raise interest rates.

If the government budget shifts to a surplus, that adds to the supply of loanable funds, which tends to lower interest rates. It was no surprise to those of us who stress money that enactment of the surtax was followed by a decline in interest rates. That's precisely what we had predicted and what our analysis leads us to predict. But—and

I come to the main point—in my opinion, the state of the budget by itself has no significant effect on the course of nominal income, on inflation, on deflation, or on cyclical fluctuations.

The crucial words in these statements are "by itself" because the whole problem of interpretation is precisely that you are always having changes in monetary policy and that you are always having changes in fiscal policy. And if you want to think clearly about the two separately, you must somehow try to separate the influence of fiscal policy from the influence of monetary policy. The question you want to ask yourself is, "Is what happened to the government budget the major factor that produced a particular change, or is it what happened to monetary variables?"

I recognize, of course, that there is no unique way to separate monetary policy from fiscal policy, but I think there would be wide agreement on the part of most people that by fiscal policy we mean changes in the relation of taxes to spending, and that by monetary policy, we mean changes in certain monetary totals. Some people might want to use as the relevant monetary total the monetary base; some people might want to use the money supply in the sense of currency and demand deposits; some people might want to use a broader money supply.

For the moment, those differences do not matter. What matters is that we ask the question, "What happens if you hold monetary policy constant and you change fiscal policy?" Or, "What happens if you hold fiscal policy constant and you change monetary policy?" Analytically—I'm going to discuss the statistical evidence later—we can separate monetary and fiscal policy by considering a situation in which monetary policy proceeds in a certain way, and we hypothetically consider a big tax increase or a big tax cut. What difference would that make?

In talking about fiscal policy, when I discuss the relation of taxes and expenditures, I don't mean current tax receipts and current payments, because all of us would agree that that's not solely a question of policy, but partly a result of what happens to the economy. Currently, about the best measure of fiscal policy is to be found in something like the high-employment budget, in the notion of what taxes and expenditures would be at high levels of employment.

I was delighted to see the Council of Economic Advisers, under Walter Heller's chairmanship, follow up the suggestion which had been made in 1947 by the Committee for Economic Development, and independently by me, that we look at fiscal policy in terms of the high-employment budget.[3] The Council provided for the first time some very useful and interesting figures on fiscal policy by itself, namely, on the state of the high-employment budget.

Now it's perfectly clear that fiscal policy can change by itself without a change in monetary policy. You can have a tax cut, let us say, and finance the resulting deficit by borrowing from the market. If you do that, that will have an effect on interest rates, but the money supply need not be affected. Alternatively, the change in fiscal policy can be accompanied by a change in monetary policy. You can have a tax cut and finance the deficit by printing money.

The essence of the pure fiscal position is that it doesn't make any difference which of those you do. The essence of the monetary position that I'm presenting is that it makes an enormous difference which of those you do, that those two kinds of tax cut will have very different effects. That's what I mean by separating the effect of fiscal policy by itself, from the effect of monetary policy by itself.

The fascinating thing to me is that the widespread faith

in the potency of fiscal policy—this is flying straight in the face of some words that Walter Heller spoke a few moments ago when he talked about the proven effectiveness of fiscal policy—rests on no evidence whatsoever. It's based on pure assumption. It's based on a priori reasoning.

I'll come back to that point of available evidence a little later and document it more fully. But it is worth dealing briefly with the a priori argument, I think—the argument from first principles—because at first it seems so persuasive. And the question is, "What's wrong with it?" It certainly seems obvious that if you raise taxes, as you did with the surtax, that clearly reduces the disposable income of the people who pay the taxes, leaves them with less to spend, and reduces spending. Surely, that is anti-inflationary. What could be clearer and simpler? How could any fool in his right mind deny so obvious a chain of events?

The trouble is that what I've said so far is only half the story. There's another half to it which is typically left out. If the federal government imposes a surtax, as it did, but keeps on spending roughly the same amount of money, as it did, then that reduces the amount it has to borrow. If it raises $10 billion more in taxes, it now has to borrow $10 billion less. The taxpayers have less money, but the people who would have loaned the government the funds with which to finance their spending have more.

So, you have to ask, "What happens to that $10 billion which the government otherwise would have borrowed?" The answer is that that $10 billion is now available for people to use to pay their taxes with or for people to lend to others. That's why the interest rate can be predicted to fall. The tax increase does reduce the demand for loanable funds on the part of the government. That lowers the interest rate. But the reduction in the interest rate induces somebody else to come and borrow those funds that otherwise would have been available for the government.

It provides the possibility of greater private investment, expenditure on housing, whatever it may be that people are borrowing it for. And so, if you take both sides of the picture to a first approximation, there's a standoff. Taxpayers have $10 billion less, and the people who would have loaned that money to the government have $10 billion more. If there is going to be any net effect, it has to be on a more sophisticated level; it has to be the indirect effect of the reduction in interest rates on other variables. In particular, it has to be a willingness on the part of the populace to hold more money, more nominal money, when the interest rate goes down.

I only sketch this—it isn't intended to be a full analysis— to show that on a purely theoretical level, you cannot come out with a clean case. It could be that fiscal policy is still potent. I don't mean to say that, in abstract theory, these indirect effects could not be strong. Keynes thought they were. And you can perfectly well establish an entirely correct theoretical chain of reasoning whereby those indirect effects would be strong. It is possible, but it's not obvious. And so you have to look at facts. When you look at facts, there's a strong tendency to be anecdotal. After all, it's much more appealing to look at particular episodes. They are more dramatic. They are more immediately accessible. And, especially, when we talk rather than write, they fit into the mode of discourse much better.

There's nothing wrong with doing that. Those individual episodes are relevant evidence, and they are useful to look at—I'm going to look at some—but they are a very small part of the evidence. If we are really going to examine the evidence, we want to look at experience over a long period we want to look at all the experience, we want to look at the average effect. One swallow doesn't make a spring; one case of confirmation or disconfirmation doesn't settle anything.

I think it will be interesting if you have an experiment in 1969 on the effects of fiscal versus monetary policy. But whichever way it goes, it's only going to be a small part of the total body of accumulated evidence that is available. But let me turn to a couple of episodes.

The one that is most dramatic and that Walter Heller emphasized most is, of course, the 1964 tax cut. Now let me point out to you that, so far as I know, there has been no empirical demonstration that that tax cut had any effect on the total flow of income in the U. S. There has been no demonstration that if monetary policies had been maintained unchanged—I'll come back to that in a moment—the tax cut would have been really expansionary on nominal income. It clearly made interest rates higher than they otherwise would have been. But there is no evidence that by itself it was expansionary on income.

Arthur Okun wrote a paper in the summer of 1965 that he presented at the Statistical Association Meeting that fall which gave a statistical analysis of the effect of the tax cut.[4] It's a very interesting paper; it's a fine thing to have done. I think we ought to have more such examinations. But if you examine what he did, you will find that what he has is an illustrative calculation of, not evidence on, the importance of the tax cut.

What Okun did was to assume away the whole problem because he looked only at the effect of fiscal policy without asking what role monetary policy played during that period. What he did was to say that we could put monetary policy aside, because interest rates didn't change during the period and that, therefore, we could suppose that monetary policy was neutral. As I've just made clear, that really begs the fundamental issue. If monetary policy were really neutral, you would have expected interest rates to go up, not stay constant. You had a tax cut. That meant the government had to borrow more, which would have raised interest rates. If, despite that effect, interest rates didn't go up, monetary policy must have been doing something.

What Art Okun did in that paper was to say: Let us assume that the theory underlying fiscal policy is correct. Then what do the figures say about the numerical value of the multiplier in this episode. He did not present evidence on whether that theory is correct.

To do that, you need to see what happened to money separately. If you look at what happened to money, you will find that the temporal pattern of money supply conforms much better to the temporal pattern of nominal income than does the tax cut. There was a decided tapering off in the growth of money supply in early 1962 through about the first three-quarters of '62. This was reflected in the last part of '62 and early '63 by a tapering off in the economy. You then had a switch in monetary policy. It became more expansive—the quantity of money started growing—and lo and behold, about six or nine or ten months later, before the tax cut had taken effect, income started to rise at a more rapid rate.

In order to make the tax cut responsible for that, you have to argue that anticipation of the tax cut produced an increase in income, and that then, after you had the tax cut, despite the fact that it had been anticipated, it had its full effect all over again. So that episode, while it's a nice dramatic episode, does not, as it has so far been analyzed, provide much evidence.

From what I've said so far, I haven't proved that the tax cut didn't have an expansionary effect. I'm not trying to argue that it has been established conclusively that fiscal policy had no effect in that episode alone. I'm only saying that so far, there is no persuasive statistical, empirical evaluation which gives you reason to say that it had an effect.

1966–1967 is a nice episode. It is a nice controlled experiment. Nature happened to turn one out. In early 1966, April 1966, the Federal Reserve stepped very hard on the monetary brake. The quantity of money, however you measure it, slowed down its rate of growth very sharply. The narrow definition actually declined; the broader definition increased from April to December, but at a much slower pace than it had before. During that same period, the high-employment budget moved toward a larger and larger deficit.

If you were to look at the high-employment budget alone, you would say that we should have had a boom in the early part of 1967. If you were to look at monetary policy alone, you would say that we should have had a slowdown in the early part of 1967. Well, as Walter testified in his talk, we did have a slowdown in the early part of 1967, as you would have expected from the monetary influence, in contrast to what you would have expected from the fiscal influence.

Early in 1967, the Fed turned around, and it is true, as Walter pointed out, that 1967—I guess he was saying '68, but '67 too—comes pretty close to being a record year of monetary expansion. And about six to nine months after the Fed turned around, the economy turned around. We started to have an expanded growth in nominal income.

As for the 1969 possible experiment, it's too soon to say because I do not think that you ought to judge fiscal policy, as you ought not to judge monetary policy, on whether it has an overnight influence of major magnitude. There are lags involved in fiscal policy, as there are in monetary policy. Whether you have an experiment or not depends on how the Federal Reserve behaves. The various monetary totals have been behaving in very different ways, for reasons about which maybe I'll have a chance to say something later. At the moment I'll put it to one side. If the Fed should continue with a very easy policy, of the kind that it had prior to the past two months, that is, if the rate of growth of the money supply defined broadly should continue at its present pace, and if the rate of growth of the narrow money supply should step up and come closer to its usual relation with the rate of growth of the broader money supply, then that would suggest that you would not have a slowdown in the early part of '69.

On the other hand, the fiscal effect would suggest that you would. So you might have another experiment. But whether you do or not, depends on what the Fed does. If the Fed should repeat its behavior of early 1966, if it should step on the brake very hard, then both fiscal and monetary policy will be going in the same direction and you will not have an experiment. But, as I said before, none of this is very satisfactory. This is all episodic. What you need is systematic evidence that takes account of other factors at work, that tries to examine what happens not only at certain critical points of time, but throughout a longer period.

The interesting thing is that those people who speak most loudly about the potency of fiscal policy have produced no such evidence. But there is a great deal of evidence which has been produced primarily by those of us who have argued for the potency of monetary policy. You know, it is always being said that we are unrealistic, that we are abstract and so on. But I think that there is no one who can deny that we have, in the course of the past fifteen years, accumulated an enormous amount of empirical evidence on the questions that are at issue. I'd like to call your attention to some items in that list which are relevant to the particular issue of the potency of fiscal and monetary policy.

I'm going to run over them very hastily. Some sixteen years ago, I wrote an article that compared the Civil War to World War I and World War II. The particular question I asked was, "Do you get a better understanding of what happened to prices during those three wars by looking at what was happening to monetary magnitudes, or by looking at what was happening to fiscal magnitudes?" [5] The answer was completely unambiguous. And nobody has since produced any evidence contradicting that analysis. It turns out that you get a very clear, straight-forward interpretation of price behavior in those three wars by looking at monetary magnitudes; you do not get an explanation by looking at fiscal magnitudes.

Second, Walter Heller was kind enough to comment on the studies that Anna Schwartz and I have done under the auspices of the National Bureau of Economic Research. We have studied the relation between monetary magnitude and economic magnitudes over the course of a hundred years, roughly a century. During that period, fiscal policy changed enormously. At the beginning of that period, the government budget was negligible. In the period since World War II, the government budget has been mammoth. And yet we found roughly the same kind of a relationship between monetary and economic magnitudes over the whole of that one-hundred–year period.

If fiscal policy were playing a dominant influence, it

should have introduced more variability, as Walter properly said it should have, into the relation between money and income in the later part than in the earlier; but as far as we can see, it's a homogeneous universe.

Third, some years back David Meiselman and I published a study directed specifically at the question, "Do monetary magnitudes or autonomous expenditure magnitudes give you a better interpretation of the movements in nominal income over short periods of time?" [6] That article produced a great controversy and a large number of replies and counterreplies.[7] It's a matter of biblical exegesis to trace through the thrusts and counterthrusts of that controversy though I am sure it would be good for all your souls to do so.

But one thing that came out of that controversy is that everybody agreed that the monetary magnitudes did have an important and systematic influence. The complaint that was made against us was the one that Walter makes tonight, that we had gone too far in denying that the autonomous magnitudes exerted an influence.

The most recent study is one by the Federal Reserve Bank of St. Louis,[8] which Walter was good enough to refer to as an unofficial arm of the Chicago School—well, we ought to have one out of twelve anyway. It is an extremely thorough and very fascinating study in which they have related quarter-to-quarter changes in GNP to changes in monetary totals over prior quarters and also to changes in governmental expenditures and taxes. They have been very thorough. Anything that anybody suggested to them which might be wrong with what they initially did, they have tried out. As a result, they have tried out many of the possible permutations and combinations. They have tried the high-employment budget and they have tried other budget concepts. But I'll refer to their findings about the high-employment budget.

What they have done is to try to see whether the monetary or the fiscal magnitudes play a more consistent and systematic role in explaining the course of GNP change over the period 1952 to 1968. That is the right period because Walter Heller is right in pointing to the Federal Reserve-Treasury Accord of 1951 as marking a distinct change in the role of monetary policy and its possibility.

Let me quote their summary conclusion. They say, "This section tested the propositions that the response of economic activity to fiscal actions relative to monetary actions is (I) larger, (II) more predictable, and (III) faster." [9]

Let me repeat this more explicitly. The proposition they tested was that the response of economic activity to fiscal action was larger, more predictable, and faster than the response of the economy to monetary action. "The results of the tests," they say, "were not consistent with any of these propositions. Consequently, either the commonly used measures of fiscal influence do not correctly indicate the degree and the direction of such influence, or there was no measurable net fiscal influence on total spending in the test period." [10] To put it in simpler terms, what they found— far from there being a proven efficiency of fiscal policy—was that, as a statistical matter, the regression coefficients of the high-employment budget surplus or deficit, if the monetary variables are held constant, were not statistically significant.

They found that if you separated expenditures from taxes and treated them separately, expenditures did have some effect but taxes had none. An expenditure increase tended to have a positive influence on income in the first two quarters after the increase, but it had a negative influence in the next two quarters.

Apparently, the expenditure increase had had a short-term

influence before it started to work its way through the credit market. Then there was the delayed effect of the half of the picture that, as I mentioned before, is generally not discussed.[11]

That's another piece of evidence. Maybe it's my myopia that leads me not to know the empirical studies the other way around. I would like to have some references to careful, systematic, empirical studies which have analyzed the influence of fiscal policy along with the influence of monetary policy, and which provide some evidence that, for a given quantity of money, or a given monetary-supply policy defined in some other way, fiscal policy has a significant influence on nominal national income and prices.[12]

Surely, I think the time has come to utter the usual poker challenge to those who maintain that fiscal effects are important for inflation and the price level. It seems to me that it is time they put up and gave us some evidence to support the repeated assertions to that effect.

Reply

WALTER W. HELLER

It is difficult to work up anger or even indignation in a discussion or debate with Milton Friedman. He is always so charming and disarming, even when he's dead wrong! Listening to Milton, I was reminded of a postcard I got in Washington from a Montana observer, whose message was, "Don't you go getting reasonable with me while I'm busy getting mad at you."

I'd be the first to admit that not enough has been done to isolate and measure the impact of fiscal policy. So far as I know, we have no evidence consisting of a simple (or, for that matter, esoteric) one-equation correlation between fiscal actions and the level of economic activity. Yet, even apart from the impressive correlation between fiscal activism and high employment, we have also had a series of experiences on the firing line in which the predicted consequences of specific fiscal actions—or failures to act—became the actual consequences (within quite tolerable margins of error). Not, mind you, a perfect record, but a very respectable batting average.

But beyond this, Milton's complaint that fiscal policy is pure theory that has never been tested would certainly come as a surprise to the many top-notch econometricians who have, in one way or another, been doing that ever since the Keynesian revolution started three decades ago.

Again, it's true that they may not have asked, in their research, the exact question in the exact way that Milton Friedman has in mind. Indeed, those who are doing this work—especially those who are using complete models of the economy as in the Brookings-SSRC model and the Federal Reserve-MIT model—are persuaded that one needs to go far beyond a one-equation system to get reasonably reliable and balanced results.

They are testing what they regard as more advanced, better formulated, and more interesting questions than the simple one of whether fiscal or monetary policy is paramount. Yet, along the way, they have been substantiating the importance of *both* fiscal and monetary policy. And they are devoting a lot of time to refining the specification of the fiscal and monetary policy sectors on the sensible grounds that one cannot test and measure the effects of policy on the economy without a very carefully and correctly specified model. I hardly need add that these studies all show that fiscal policy matters a great deal.

Turning from defense to attack, I also think that one should be aware of the very interesting "hindcasts" or "backcasts" that have been made using the monetarists' demand-for-money equation. *Ex post* correlations, after all, are not enough. A key test of any given theory and set of findings is a reasonable ability to forecast on the basis of the variables identified as critical by such theory and research. Comparing actual changes in nominal income with those predicted by, say, Milton's money-demand equation does not lead to impressive results. Though I don't have the details at hand, I recall that comparisons made on this basis demonstrate that the monetarists have no corner on good (or bad) forecasting.[1]

Further, I suppose I shouldn't let the 1964 tax cut go entirely unmentioned in these comments even though the gulf between us is so obvious, so wide, that there is no real possibility of reconciling our positions. First, let me repeat that I don't see how the economy could have climbed to full employment under the incubus of a $12 to $13 billion full-employment surplus. Given the balance of payments and other constraints of the real world, the idea that monetary policy would have been capable of generating a matching amount of private investment—in order to reach a savings-investment relationship consistent with full employment—is next to inconceivable. And surely, the monetary policy prevailing at the time (which allegedly did the whole job) had no such power. The tax cut was the critical motive force.

The tax-cut issue is so important that I can't just leave it at that. I have to take a closer look at the record, since Professor Friedman has not done it justice.

It is true that GNP started accelerating in the second half of 1963, before the tax cut took effect. It is also true that this surge was mainly fueled by sharp increases in business-capital spending—by the way, both casual observation and penetrating study have shown this surge to be related to the tax incentives provided in 1962. Monetary policy also helped—without the credit expansion that occurred, the rising demand from the investment-goods sector could not have been as fully met.

But it is in consumption behavior—the most directly and immediately responsive spending sector in any fiscal policy model—that one can most readily identify tax-cut effects. In the three quarters preceding the tax cut, consumption spending grew an average of $4.4 billion per quarter. For the three quarters following the cut, the average jumped to $8.4 billion per quarter—not a bad response (and close to forecasts).

The relationships between the tax cut and the ensuing jump in economic activity are examined in some detail in the paper by Arthur Okun, the present Chairman of the Council of Economic Advisers, to which Milton referred. Surprisingly enough, my view of it differs from Milton's. As I see it, Okun's appraisal provides further impressive, even if not conclusive, evidence of the expansionary impact of the tax cut.[2]

Now, what about 1966–67? Milton says that by our lights —that is, by the lights of the "new economists"—we should have forecast a continuing boom throughout 1967. But he is wide of the mark. I cannot agree that one of my persuasion—however Friedman describes it—would have predicted a boom in 1967. I'm widely on record (through my Bank Letter for the National City Bank of Minneapolis) with a forecast of a $42-billion GNP gain for 1967. The actual increase turned out to be $42 billion. Professor Friedman is widely on record, through such instruments as his *Newsweek* articles and his NET telecast early in 1967, with dark (and qualitative) forebodings of recession. Unemployment in 1967 averaged 3.8 per cent, the same as in 1966, and was narrowly above 4 per cent only in September and October—an unlikely picture of recession. But I have yet to see the monetarists admit to their error in reading the monetary tea leaves for 1967. After all, there was a slow-down, and one could (and they did) call it a mini-recession —and so, in retrospect, although their widely predicted recession failed to materialize, somehow, they see the money-supply theory as calling the shots rather nicely.

Just as there was no occasion for predicting a recession, surely, the developments in the full-employment surplus in 1966–67 provided no occasion for predicting a boom. Reading from a table published by the Federal Reserve Bank of St. Louis, I find that the full-employment surplus was hovering near zero in the first three quarters of 1966. Coupling that with the fact that the Fed had slammed on the brakes in the absence of appropriate fiscal action, I find it entirely reasonable that the forecaster taking a *balanced* fiscal and monetary view would foresee a slowdown in the first half of 1967. At the same time, with the full-employment deficit leaping upward late in 1966, at the same time that the Federal Reserve moved its foot from the brake to the accelerator, it was quite reasonable to forecast, as we correctly did, a sharp upswing later in 1967.

Further, a realistic forecaster had to plug policy—personified by President Lyndon Johnson—into his forecast. I have sometimes said that the U. S. economy would not have a recession while Lyndon Johnson was President. It wouldn't dare! In the face of the early 1967 slowdown, he released budget funds he had impounded; he called for restoration of the investment credit; he released mortgage moneys; and so on. It was reasonable—and right—to plug Lyndon Johnson into the forecast. Now I don't know what Milton will do with that.

Another point on which Milton jousts with caricature is in asserting that those who lean towards the fiscal approach make the mistake of assuming that the way in which a

deficit is financed will not alter the consequences of the
fiscal action that produces the deficit. Breathes there a fiscalist so pure as to take this illogical position, long since
exposed in even the most elementary of economics text-
books? I doubt it.[3]

Let me say again that what we apparently need is an
"economists' disarmament agreement," a recognition by each
side of the potential merit in the other side's position rather
than a continuation of the divisive and counterproductive
indoor sport of sniping at each other's conclusions. It would
hardly be a happy upshot of the debate if Friedman and
the monetarists convinced you that fiscal policy and discretion won't work while Heller and the "new economists" persuaded you that the money-supply thesis and rigid rules are
the road to ruin.

Yet, I must confess that in this attempt at de-escalation,
we've sent a number of notes to Hanoi, spelled Chicago,
offering to stop the bombing and negotiate a settlement,
looking to a working coalition with the Viet Cong. But the
reply has been stern and stony: stop the bombing in the
North and withdraw completely from the South, and *then*
we'll negotiate.

Reply

MILTON FRIEDMAN

I am delighted to have the Johnson theory of the business cycle added to monetary theories, real theories, "x" theories, and so on. I want to comment on some of the points that Walter made initially and try to answer some of the questions he raised. I think that I might very well start with a point he made before and which he repeated now. He said that he would like us to stop being asymmetrical about tax increases or tax cuts on the one hand, and expenditure decreases on the other.

I want to make it clear that I have never favored expenditure decreases as a stabilization device. I agree with Walter that it would be inconsistent, completely inconsistent, for me to argue that tax increases and decreases are ineffective in stemming inflation or promoting expansion, but that spending decreases or increases are effective. That would be a silly position and, as far as I know, I have never taken it, though maybe I've been careless in what I have written and have given a misleading impression. I have been in favor of tax decreases and expenditure decreases in 1964, in 1966, and in 1968, but not for stabilization purposes. I am in favor of expenditure decreases from a long-range point of view because I think that the U. S. federal budget is too large compared to what we're getting for it. We're not getting our money's worth out of it. And, therefore, I would like to see government spending brought down. I have not argued— at least, if I have, I will immediately admit that I should not have and I don't know of any quotation in which I have (if Walter has any, I hope he will give them to me)—that expenditure decreases are a way to achieve stabilization at a time of inflationary pressure.

I have said something different. I have said that, from the point of view of the fiscalists, a tax increase or expenditure decrease are equivalent. And, therefore, I have often said that if you are going to adopt the policy of the fiscalist, I would rather see you adopt it through expenditure decreases than through tax increases. But I personally have never argued that that is an effective stabilization device, and I don't believe that it is.

Let me turn to some of the specific issues that Walter raised in his first discussion and see if I can clarify a few points that came up.

First of all, the question is, Why do we look only at the money stock? Why don't we also look at interest rates? Don't you have to look at both quantity and price? The answer is yes, but the interest rate is not the price of money in the sense of the money stock. The interest rate is the price of credit. The price of money is how much goods and services you have to give up to get a dollar. You can have

big changes in the quantity of money without any changes
in credit. Consider for a moment the 1848–58 period in the
United States. We had a big increase in the quantity of
money because of the discovery of gold. This increase didn't,
in the first instance, impinge on the credit markets at all.

You must sharply distinguish between money in the sense
of the money or credit market, and money in the sense of the
quantity of money. And the price of money in that second
sense is the inverse of the price level—not the interest rate.
The interest rate is the price of credit. As I mentioned earlier,
the tax increase we had would tend to reduce the price of
credit because it reduces the demand for credit, even though
it didn't affect the money supply at all.

So I do think you have to look at both price and quantity.
But the price you have to look at from this point of view
is the price level, not the interest rate.

Next, he said that 1967 was the easiest money year since
1962. Yet there was a big rise in interest rates. In other con-
nections, I have argued that our researches show that a
rapid increase in the quantity of money tends to lower
interest rates only for a brief period—about six months.
After that, it tends to raise interest rates. Conversely, a slow
rate of increase in the quantity of money tends to raise
interest rates only for about six months, and after that, it
tends to lower them.[1]

If you ask where in the world interest rates are highest,
the answer is in Brazil, Chile, places like that where the
quantity of money has been going up like mad. Interest
rates in the U. S. fell dramatically from 1929 to 1933. The
quantity of money declined by a third. So it's not a surprise
to us that you could have the quantity of money easy in the
sense of quantity, and interest rates rise or fall or do almost

anything else.

Next, he asks, "Which of the Friedmans do you believe—the one who stresses permanent-income relationships or the one who stresses the close causal connection?" Well, belive both of them if you take them at what they said. The permanent-income analysis has to do with the demand for real money balances, and it was an analysis that was based on annual data covering decades. There is no Friedman who has argued that there is an immediate, mechanical, causal connection between changes in the quantity of money and changes in income.

What I have always argued is that there is a connection which is, on the average, close but which may be quite variable in an individual episode. I have emphasized that the inability to pin down the lag means that there are lots of factors about which I'm ignorant. That doesn't mean that money doesn't have a systematic influence. But it does mean that there is a good deal of variability in the influence.

The data support the view that a 1 per cent change in the rate of expansion of the quantity of money tends to produce, on the average, a 2 per cent change in the rate of growth of nominal income. There is a big multiplier, as the permanent income analysis would lead you to expect. And there is a cyclical relation. I'm sorry, but I really don't see any inconsistency between the position I've taken on these two points.

Next, Walter Heller asks, Which of the money supplies do you want? M_1 or M_2? Which quantity of money do you want to use? A perfectly reasonable and appropriate and proper question and I'm glad to answer it. In almost all cases, it makes no difference. The only time it makes a difference is when our silly Regulation Q gets in the way. We have a Regulation Q that pegs the maximum rate that commercial banks can pay on time deposits. Whenever you either hit that Regulation-Q limit or you come through from the other side, the two monetary totals diverge and tell you different stories, and you cannot trust either one.

At all other times, you will very seldom find that the message told to you by M_1 is much different than the message told to you by M_2. So what I say in answer to this is that if we can only get rid of that silly Regulation Q, which is introducing all the noise into the system, then I will let you choose: you take whichever one of those monetary totals you want and I will be willing to accept that choice. Of course, it would be even better if you also abolished the prohibition of payment of interest on demand deposits, because that also has been a factor that has produced a discrepancy between these two monetary totals.

Then there was all this talk about being locked into a rigid rule. You know, I have always found it a good rule of thumb that when somebody starts resorting to metaphors, there is something wrong with his argument.

When you start talking about cars driving along a road, and whether you want to lock the steering wheel, well that's a good image; the automatic pilot, I agree, is a good one. But metaphors or similes are to remind you of arguments; they are not a substitute for an argument.

The reason I believe that you would do better with a fixed rule, with a constant rate of increase in the quantity of money, is because I have examined U. S. experience with discretionary monetary policy. I have gone back and have asked, as I reexamine this period, "Would the U. S. have been better off or worse off if we had had a fixed rule?" I challenge anybody to go back over the monetary history of the United States, and come out with any other conclusion than that for the great bulk of the time, you would have been better off with the fixed rule. You would clearly have avoided all the major mistakes.

The reason why that doesn't rigidly lock you in, in the sense in which Walter was speaking, is that I don't believe that money is all that matters. The automatic pilot is the price system. It isn't perfectly flexible, it isn't perfectly free, but it has a good deal of capacity to adjust. If you look at what happened to this country when we adjusted to post-World War II, to the enormous decline in our expenditures, and the shift in the direction of resources, you have to say that we did an extraordinarily effective job of adjusting, and that this is because there is an automatic pilot.

But if an automatic pilot is going to work, if you're going to have the market system work, it has to have some basic, stable framework. It has to have something it can count on. And the virtue of a fixed rule, of a constant rate of increase in the quantity of money, is that it would provide such a stable monetary framework. I have discussed that many times in many different ways, and I really have nothing to add.

Let me only say two additional things. I meant to say earlier, with reference to putting yourself down on paper as far as predictions are concerned—I will give Walter Heller a bibliographical note and he can check—that Prentice-Hall recently brought out (this is a free advertisement) a collection of some essays of mine called *Dollars and Deficits*.[2] These are papers directed at a general audience and contain more popular things including a couple of memoranda that I wrote at various times for meetings of the Federal Reserve Board. I think that if you look through these, you will find that they contain a considerable number of forecasts.

I have some footnotes at various points indicating what did happen later. Some of the forecasts are pretty good, some aren't; but you can judge for yourself whether you think that, on the whole, the record is good or bad.

The final thing I want to talk about is the statement that Walter made at the end of his initial talk, when he said, Look at the world economy; hasn't it been far healthier during post-World War II than it was between the Wars? Of course. It certainly has been enormously healthier. Why? Well, again, I'm sorry to have to be consistent, but in 1953, I gave a talk in Stockholm, which is also reprinted in that collection of papers, under the title of "Why the American Economy is Depression Proof."

I think that I was right, that as of that time and as of today, the American economy is depression proof. The reasons I gave at that time did not include the fact that discretionary monetary and fiscal policy was going to keep things on an even keel. I believe that the reason why the world has done so much better, the reason why we haven't had any depressions in that period, is not because of the positive virtue of the fine tuning that has been followed, but because we have avoided the major mistakes of the interwar period. Those major mistakes were the occasionally severe deflations of the money stock.

We did learn something from the Great Depression. We learned that you do not have to cut the quantity of money by a third over three or four years. We learned that you ought to have numbers on the quantity of money. If the Federal Reserve System in 1929 to 1933 had been publishing statistics on the quantity of money, I don't believe that the Great Depression could have taken the course it did. There were no numbers. And we have not since then, and we will not in the foreseeable future, permit a monetary authority to make the kind of mistake that our monetary authorities made in the 30's.

That, in my opinion, is the major reason why we have had such a different experience in post-World War II.

Notes

Is Monetary Policy Being Oversold?
Walter W. Heller

1. Anyone interested in the ongoing debate about monetary policy should read Professor Tobin's piece in *The Washington Post* for April 16, 1967 (which, in the best journalistic tradition, was printed under the headline, "Tobin Attacks Friedman's Theories of Money Supply"), and Dr. Gramley's article, "The Informational Content of Interest Rates as Indicators of Monetary Policy," in *Proceedings: 1968 Money and Banking Workshop,* Federal Reserve Bank of Minneapolis (May, 1968). (A companion article, "Interest Rates Versus the Quantity of Money: The Policy Issues," by Professor Phillip Cagan, is also well worth reading.) More technical criticisms of Professor Friedman's position will be found in two papers, the first by Professor Tobin: "Money and Income: Post Hoc Propter Hoc," which is available in mimeograph. The second is by Professors Michael Lovell and Edward Prescott: "Money, Multiplier-Accelerator Interaction and the Business Cycle," *Southern Journal of Economics,* July, 1968.

2. "U.S. Financial Data, week ending November 6, 1968," Federal Reserve Bank of St. Louis, p. 1.

3. Gramley, *op. cit.,* p. 23.

4. This was not only Keynes's view; it is, I believe, Milton Friedman's. Indeed, his formulation of the monetary process—of the process whereby a change in the supply of money works its potent magic—reads remarkably like Tobin's, or for that matter, like Keynes's. See, for example, his "Money and Business Cycles," p. 60. This paper was written with Mrs. Schwartz, and appeared in the February, 1963 issue of the *Review of Economics and Statistics.*

5. Milton Friedman and Anna Jacobson Schwartz, *A Monetary History of the United States: 1867–1960* (Princeton, N.J.: Princeton University Press, 1963), p. 682.

6. An unpublished paper by the staff of the St. Louis Federal Reserve Bank cited by Professor Friedman in support of the contrary position (see pp. 60–62) was not available to me at

the time of this debate, but has since been published. (Leonall Anderson and Jerry Jordan, "Monetary and Fiscal Actions: A Test of Their Relative Importance in Economic Stabilization," St. Louis Federal Reserve Bank *Review*, November, 1968.) It calls for comment, especially since it has been much praised by the monetarists. It concludes, in effect, that monetary policy matters greatly and fiscal policy little, if at all. But a faulty specification of the world cannot lead to correct conclusions. And the Anderson-Jordan specification is faulty in pursuing strictly one-way economics:

• They make no allowance for reverse causation, for the influence of economic activity on the money supply. Yet such causation was clearly at work in the 1952–68 period they cover.

• Similarly, they do not allow for the influence of economic activity on government spending. Yet where demand expansion generates inflation, real government spending may be treated as an exogenous variable, but nominal spending surely cannot.

On the first point, suffice it to note that during much of the 1952–68 period, the Federal Reserve adhered to what has been called the "free-reserves doctrine." Under this decision rule, money supply became, in part, a dependent variable, for example:

• When the level of interest rates had to be fixed with an eye to our external position so that changes in the level of economic activity had to be "taken up," so to speak, in the stock of money.

• When the level of interest rates had to be held down to avoid thwarting the stimulus of the 1964 tax cut so that, here also, the money supply had to follow the lead of nominal GNP, i.e., had to respond to changes in economic activity rather than vice versa.

7. Milton Friedman, *A Program for Monetary Stability* (New York: Fordham University Press, 1959), p. 87.

8. Organization for Economic Cooperation and Development, *Fiscal Policy for a Balanced Economy*, Paris, 1968, p. 23. This report reviews and appraises the fiscal policy experiences of Belgium, France, Germany, Italy, Sweden, the United Kingdom,

and the United States since 1955 and makes recommendations for improving the operation of fiscal policy. See also the companion volume by Bent Hansen, *Fiscal Policy in Seven Countries*, OECD, Paris, 1969, which presents in detail the results of the econometric studies underlying some of the conclusions of the experts' report.

9. I reviewed a number of the issues involved in this controversy in my article, "CED's Stabilizing Budget Policy After Ten Years," *The American Economic Review*, September, 1957, pp. 634–651.

Has Fiscal Policy Been Oversold?
Milton Friedman

1. Milton Friedman, "The Supply of Money and Changes in Prices and Output," *The Relationship of Prices to Economic Stability and Growth*, 85th Cong., 2nd Sess., Joint Committee Print (Washington, D. C., U. S. Government Printing Office, 1958), pp. 241–256, quotation from pp. 255–256. To be reprinted in Milton Friedman, *The Optimum Quantity of Money and Other Essays* (Chicago, Ill.: Aldine Publishing Co., 1969).

2. Contained in the 1962, 1963, and 1964 *Economic Report of the President*, (Washington, D. C.: U. S. Government Printing Office, 1962, 1963, 1964).

3. *Taxes and the Budget: A Program for Prosperity in a Free Economy*, a statement by the Research and Policy Committee of the Committee for Economic Development (November, 1947); Milton Friedman, "A Monetary and Fiscal Framework for Economic Stability," *American Economic Review*, XXXVIII (June, 1948), p. 249 (originally presented before Econometric Society in September, 1947). The concept that has come to be called the high-employment budget, I labelled, in my paper, the "stable" budget, and the council first labelled, in its 1962 Report, the "full-employment" budget (*op. cit.*, p. 80).

4. Arthur M. Okun, "Measuring the Impact of the 1964 Tax Reduction," in Walter W. Heller (ed.), *Perspectives on Economic Growth* (New York: Random House, 1968).

5. "Price, Income, and Monetary Changes in Three Wartime Periods," *American Economic Review* (May, 1952), pp. 612–625. To be reprinted in *The Optimum Quantity of Money and Other Essays, op. cit.*

6. Milton Friedman and David Meiselman, "The Relative Stability of Monetary Velocity and the Investment Multiplier in the United States, 1897–1958," *Stabilization Policies* (Commission on Money and Credit, Englewood Cliffs, N. J.: Prentice-Hall, 1963), pp. 165–268.

7. Donald D. Hester, "Keynes and the Quantity Theory: A Comment on the Friedman-Meiselman CMC Paper," and Milton Friedman and David Meiselman, "Reply to Donald Hester," *The Review of Economics and Statistics*, XLVI (November, 1964), pp. 364–377; Albert Ando and Franco Modigliani, "The Relative Stability of Monetary Velocity and the Investment Multiplier," Michael De Prano and Thomas Mayer, "Tests of the Relative Importance of Autonomous Expenditures and Money," and Milton Friedman and David Meiselman, "Reply to Ando and Modigliani and to De Prano and Mayer," *American Economic Review*, LV (September, 1965), pp. 693–792.

8. Leonall C. Anderson and Jerry L. Jordan, "Monetary and Fiscal Actions: A Test of Their Relative Importance in Economic Stabilization," *Review*, Federal Reserve Bank of St. Louis, November, 1968, pp. 11–23.

9. *Ibid.*, p. 22.

10. *Ibid.*, p. 22

11. In a footnote to his paper added after our interchange (note 6, p. 83 above), Professor Heller criticizes the St. Louis study for making no allowance for "reverse causation," i.e., for the influence of economic activity on the money supply and on government spending. The reader of the paper by Anderson and Jordan will find that they anticipate this possible criticism, discuss it explicitly, and show it to be invalid for their computations and conclusions. The key issue is to assure that, so far as possible, the variables defining monetary policy and fiscal policy are autonomous, not partly autonomous, partly induced. For

money, they achieve this by using a number of different monetary totals: the monetary base, currency plus demand deposits, currency plus all commercial bank deposits. For the government budget they do so by using high employment expenditures and receipts. For both, autonomy is reinforced by using lagged values of monetary and fiscal policy variables with different methods of allowing for lags. All variants yield essentially the same results.

Of course, no study can "prove" anything finally. Proof is reserved for logical, not empirical, propositions. What a study can do is to contradict or fail to contradict hypotheses, and even then, of course, any findings are always tentative because the evidence is necessarily incomplete and there is always the possibility that the hypothesis contradicted can be reformulated so as to be consistent with the initially contradictory evidence.

However, as a veteran of many years' standing of the kind of smoke-screen criticism levelled by Heller against the Anderson-Jordan study, I would take it far more seriously if the assertion that something may be wrong were accompanied by some evidence, empirical or analytical, that something is wrong.

12. The references added by Professor Heller in footnote 1 of his paper do not meet this challenge. They are criticisms of my work of the same kind as, though naturally more elaborate and developed than, his brief criticisms of the Anderson-Jordan article discussed in the preceding footnote. None of the criticisms gives any systematic evidence supporting the hypothesis that fiscal policy by itself has a significant influence on nominal income. To complement the references in his footnote, I should note an article of mine, "Taxes, Money and Stabilization," *Washington Post*, November 5, 1967, because it is partly in answer to several critical pieces by Tobin in the *Washington Post*, including the one referred to by Heller.

His footnote 8 gives two other references to OECD documents. Since I have not yet seen these I cannot judge whether they provide relevant empirical evidence.

Reply/Walter W. Heller

1. Gramley, who may know more about Professor Friedman's work than anyone other than Friedman himself, has compared actual yearly changes in nominal Net National Product (NNP) with those predicted by the Friedman equation as reported in "Interest Rates and the Demand for Money," *Journal of Law and Economics*, October, 1966. For the period 1948–60, the average yearly change in nominal NNP was $18.6 billion. Gramley found the average predicted changes to be $5.5 billion. It is quite true that for the period 1960–67, the two average changes are nearly identical ($37.2 billion versus $36.8 billion). But this does not contradict the point that a fixed rule ought to allow for trend changes in velocity. And if trend changes are allowed for, why not shorter run changes?

2. See Arthur M. Okun, "Measuring the Impact of the 1964 Tax Reduction," in Walter W. Heller, (ed.), *Perspectives on Economic Growth*, (New York: Random House, 1968).

3. Subsequent to our discourse in New York, I've gone over the debate Friedman and Meiselman touched off in the professional journals, which Milton summed up in his comments by indicating that everyone agreed that monetary magnitudes did have an important and systematic influence. But I find that he rather slides over the fact that, to the satisfaction of many—indeed, I think it's safe to say most—members of the profession, his own work concluding that monetary magnitudes were far more important than fiscal was effectively rebuffed.

Reply/Milton Friedman

1. For a summary of these results, see my paper "Factors Affecting the Level of Interest Rates," *1968 Proceedings*, Conference on Savings and Residential Financing (Chicago, Ill.: U. S. Savings and Loan League, 1968), pp. 11–27.

2. Milton Friedman, *Dollars and Deficits* (Englewood Cliffs, N.J.: Prentice-Hall, 1968).

3. *Ibid.*, pp. 72–96.

Glossary of Terms and References

This glossary is intended to present simple definitions and explanations of terms used by Professors Friedman and Heller in their debate. Words or phrases in italics also appear as separate entries.

Automated policy. The reliance on fixed rates of change in money and tax rates rather than frequent *discretionary* changes in *monetary* or *fiscal policy* to affect the level of economic activity. An example of automated policy is the setting of a growth rate for the *money supply* to be followed for long periods independent of current economic conditions.

Autonomous expenditures. Expenditures *exogenous* to the particular model used to forecast *GNP*. Generally regarded as autonomous are private investment, exports or net foreign balance, expenditures by the federal government or the federal deficit or the federal *full-* (or *high-*) *employment deficit,* and expenditures attributed to changes in the federal government's tax rates.

Chicago School. A name applied to a group of economists who, among other things, believe that changes in the *money supply* are a major determinant of short-run changes in the level of economic activity and the most important of the policy instruments available to the federal government for affecting short-run changes in economic activity. The members of this school generally advocate reliance upon *automated policy*.

Classical real-wage doctrine. A doctrine which holds that, in the long-run, there is no trade off between unemployment and price increases as is implied by the *Phillips curve*. It has been taken to indicate that a rising price level will not affect permanently the level of unemployment.

Committee for Economic Development (CED). A nonpartisan organization, composed of leading businessmen and educators, which issues frequent policy statements on economic matters.

Council of Economic Advisers. Three members, assisted by a professional staff of economists, who are appointed by the President to advise him on economic matters, as provided by the Employment Act of 1946.

Credit. See *Loanable Funds*.

Currency. Paper money and coins.

Demand deposits. Bank deposits legally payable upon demand and generally transferable by check.

Discretionary policy. The deliberate introduction by administrative agencies of changes in *monetary* and *fiscal policy* to serve *national economic goals*.

Easy money. A *monetary policy* regarded as stimulating economic activity. Defined by some as a policy of promoting low interest rates; by others, falling interest rates; by others, a rapid rate of growth of the quantity of money; by others an acceleration in the rate of growth of the quantity of money.

Endogenous variable. A variable whose value is determined by the values of other variables within the particular model used to explain events.

Exogenous variable. A variable whose value is determined outside the particular model used to explain events.

Federal Reserve System (Fed). The organization responsible for monetary policy in the United States. There are twelve regional federal reserve banks. The Board of Governors of the Federal Reserve System, consisting of seven governors, appointed by the President for fourteen-year terms, is the major policy-formulating group. Since 1951, its Chairman has been William McChesney Martin, Jr.

Federal Reserve-Treasury Accord. *See* Monetary Accord of 1951.

Fine tuning. The active use of *discretionary monetary* and *fiscal policy* in the attempt to offset fluctuations in the level of economic activity.

Fiscal dividend. The increase in federal revenues which results from a rise in *GNP* at any given level of tax rates.

Fiscal drag. The possible restrictive effect on the economy of the automatic growth in federal revenues arising out of the growth in *GNP*, where such revenue growth is not matched by corresponding expenditure increases and/or tax reductions. (Alternatively, fiscal drag may be defined as the growth in the potential *full-* (or *high-*) *employment surplus.*)

Fiscal policy. The use of changes in the level of taxes and expenditures (either *transfer payments* or other budget expenditures) to serve *national economic goals.*

Fiscalists. Those who believe that *fiscal policy* is the most important means available to the government for affecting the level of economic activity.

Flexible exchange rates. A situation in which exchange rates among national currencies would be free to vary in response to supply-and-demand conditions, without government attempts to maintain a fixed rate at which one currency is exchanged for another.

Forward exchange. Foreign exchange transacted for delivery at some future date.

Free reserves. The excess of *member-bank reserves* over borrowings from the *Federal Reserve System* plus reserves legally required against bank deposits.

Full (or high) employment. A situation in which all looking for jobs at the going wage rate would be able to obtain employment. For purposes of policy, because of job turnover and other frictions, full (or high) employment is currently considered to be a situation where the unemployed are only 3 or 4 per cent of the labor force.

Full- (or high-) employment surplus (deficit). A measure of the size of the surplus (deficit) which would occur in the federal government budget if the economy were at *full* (or *high*) *employment.* This concept is used because the actual amount of tax collections (and certain expenditures like unemployment compensation) is dependent upon the level of economic activity, once the government has set the tax and expenditure rates.

Gross National Product (GNP). The total value of goods and services produced in the economy within a given time period before allowance for depreciation of capital goods.

Income velocity of money. The ratio of income to the *money supply.*

Interest-rate peg. The *monetary policy* followed from 1942 to 1951 under which the *Federal Reserve System* adjusted the quantity of money so as to hold the interest rate on Treasury securities constant.

Investment tax credit. The reduction of taxes through a 7 per cent tax credit for firms purchasing new plant and equipment. First passed in 1962, it was suspended for several months in 1966–67 in an attempt to reduce such investment.

Joint Economic Committee. A Congressional committee composed of ten Senators and ten Representatives which holds hearings and issues reports on economic matters.

Liquidity preference. The desire on the part of firms and individuals to hold money.

Loanable funds. Funds that lenders are willing to make available to borrowers at a specified rate of interest.

Member-bank reserves. Currency held by banks who are members of the *Federal Reserve System,* plus their deposits at federal reserve banks.

Monetarists. Those who believe that *monetary policy* is the most important means available to the federal government for affecting the level of economic activity.

Monetary Accord of 1951. An agreement between the Treasury and the *Federal Reserve System* which ended the *interest-rate peg,* permitting *monetary policy* to respond to other objectives.

Monetary base. The sum of *member-bank reserves* and *currency* held outside banks. This is under the direct control of the *Federal Reserve System.* Between January and November 1968, the monetary base rose from $72.2 billion to $76.2 billion.

Monetary multiplier. A number giving the expected change in income per unit change in the *money supply.*

Monetary policy. The use of changes in the *money supply* and the cost and availability of credit to serve *national economic goals.*

Money supply. The total quantity of money held by the public. Two measures of the money supply are generally used. M_1 is the sum of *currency* held outside banks and *demand deposits.* M_2 is the sum of M_1 and *time deposits* held in commercial banks. Between January and November 1968, M_1 rose from $182.3 billion to $192.0 billion; M_2 from $366.4 billion to $393.9 billion (seasonally adjusted data).

Multiplier. A relationship giving the expected change in *GNP* for given changes in *autonomous expenditures.*

National economic goals. High or full employment, a satisfactory growth rate, reasonable price stability, and equilibrium in the international balance of payments. These goals are sought within a framework of economic freedom of choice and growing equality of opportunity.

New economics. A term applied to the active use of *discretionary fiscal* and *monetary policy* to serve *national economic goals.*

Nominal income. The dollar value of income. Changes in nominal income may be due to either changes in *real income* or changes in the level of prices.

Organization for Economic Cooperation and Development (OECD). An organization of twenty-two nations (from noncommunist Europe, Canada, Japan, and the United States) which was established to coordinate and advise on economic and financial policies of the member nations.

Permanent income. The average income expected to be received over a period of years.

Permanent-income hypothesis. The hypothesis that household-consumption expenditures are related to *permanent income* and not affected by deviations from this amount.

Phillips curve. A relationship between the level of unemployment and the rate of change of wages. It has been taken to indicate that it is possible to reduce unemployment only at the expense of a rising price level, so that it is necessary to trade off between reducing unemployment and holding the price level stable.

Real income. A measure of goods and services produced within a given time period. Changes in real income are computed by adjusting changes in *nominal income* for changes in the level of prices.

Real money balances. The quantity of goods and services which can be purchased from a given stock of money held by individuals. Changes in real-money balances are computed by adjusting changes in the quantity of money held for changes in the level of prices.

Real output. *See* Real income.

Regression coefficient. A statistically determined measure of the quantitative effect of a change in one factor upon another.

Regulation Q. The regulation providing the Federal Reserve Board with the power to control the interest rate paid on *time deposits* held in member commercial banks.

Surtax. A 10 per cent surcharge placed on personal and corporation income taxes passed by Congress in June 1968 and which was to be in effect for one year. It was intended to contract the level of economic activity.

Tax cut of 1964. A broad-based reduction in the personal and corporation income-tax rates passed by Congress in 1964 to reduce the size of the full-employment surplus. It was designed to expand the level of economic activity.

Tax sharing. The proposal that the federal government grant some part of its tax collections to state and local governments.

Tight money. A *monetary policy* regarded as retarding economic activity. The opposite of *easy money*.

Time deposits. Bank deposits subject to prior notice of withdrawal and not transferable by check.

Transfer payments. Payments made by the federal government to individuals, not as payments for currently productive services. These include welfare payments, unemployment compensation, and social security payments.